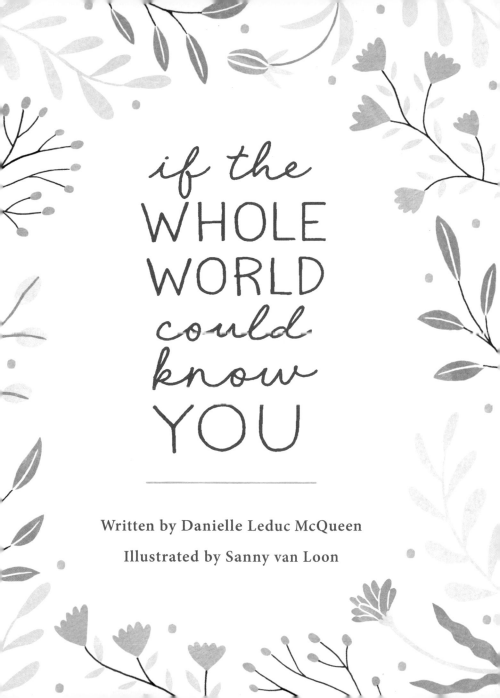

if the WHOLE WORLD could know YOU

Written by Danielle Leduc McQueen

Illustrated by Sanny van Loon

If the whole world could know you,
you'd be everyone's *favorite* person.

If everyone on this planet could meet you, they'd see you're the kind of wonderful that legends are made of,

the kind of *awesome* that we all aspire to be.

You shine your spotlight on all who surround you.
You find *fun* and *adventure* in every moment.

You do it all with such style and love
that it's incredible the seven continents
haven't yet heard your name.

If the whole world could know you,
they'd know what it's like to feel uplifted by
your *generous* and overflowing *heart*.

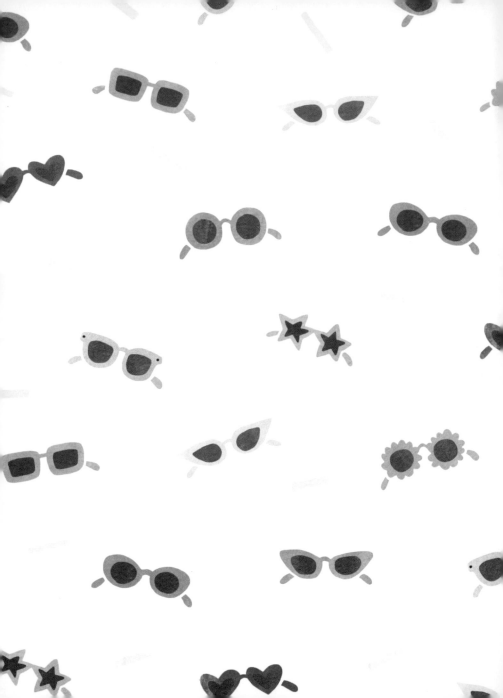

Like sweet sunshine,
you brighten the lives
of everyone you meet.

You find time and energy for all those around you, and you *truly listen* when others have something to say.

You're always there when things go sideways,

and always ready when
someone needs a hand.

You stretch life at the seams, forever giving yourself to *everything* you do, and *everyone* you know.

It's simply remarkable what you're capable of. Your passion is dazzling, your devotion electrifying.

You're not afraid of the impossible,
the fantastic, or the downright difficult.

You're the kind of person to tackle
anything with aplomb.

If the whole world could know you,
they'd marvel at your character,
and whisper in awe at your charm.

There's so much *beauty* within you,
and so much life and love in your smile.

You're radiant. You're exquisite.

You're something *extraordinary.*

If all the people on this planet could meet you, they'd be lining up to see you, clamoring over each other for a moment of your time.

You make dreary moments worth remembering
and every day worth *celebrating*.

Your *laughter* buoys even the lowest of moods.

You're every bit *exceptional,*
every ounce sensational.

You're the kind of person we all wish we could be.

If the whole world could know you,
you *wondrous* thing,
you'd be everyone's favorite person.

Because you're absolutely
magnificent. You're altogether
spectacular.

ROSE

Your magic and *sparkle*
are something to behold.

Keep shining, keep glowing, and keep doing all the *amazing* things that make you who you are...

...the rest of this planet doesn't
know what they're missing.

COMPENDIUM.
live inspired

Written by: Danielle Leduc McQueen
Illustrated by: Sanny van Loon
Art Direction by: Jessica Phoenix
Edited by: Ruth Austin

Library of Congress Control Number: 2018941324 | ISBN: 978-1-946873-37-8

3rd printing. Printed in China with soy inks on FSC®-Mix certified paper.

*Create
meaningful
moments
with gifts
that inspire.*

CONNECT WITH US
live-inspired.com | sayhello@compendiuminc.com

@compendiumliveinspired
#compendiumliveinspired